a slow dance in the flames

Lynda Monahan

a slow dance in the flames

COTEAU BOOKS

Edited by Elizabeth Philips.
Cover and book design by Duncan Campbell.
Cover illustration by Bernice Friesen.
Printed and bound in Canada.

The publisher gratefully acknowledges the financial assistance of the
Saskatchewan Arts Board, the Canada Council for the Arts,
the Department of Canadian Heritage, and the City of Regina
Arts Commission, for its publishing programme.

Coteau Books celebrates the 50th anniversary of
the Saskatchewan Arts Board with this publication.

Canadian Cataloguing in Publication Data

Monahan, Lynda, 1952
A slow dance in the flames
ISBN 1-55050-139-9

1. Title.
PS8576.045182S46 1998   C811'.54   C98-920114-7
PR9199.3.M593S46 1998

Coteau Books
401-2206 Dewdney Avenue
Regina, Saskatchewan
S4R 1H3

AVAILABLE IN THE U.S. FROM:

General Distribution Services
85 River Rock Road, Suite 202
Buffalo, New York,
USA, 14207

for Don
for Shawn, Jill, and the boys
and for Pat

with love

Contents

she came toward me in the flowing air,
a shape of change encircled by its fire.

Theodore Roethke

it is for her

it is for this child
that i write
she is about ten
tall for her age
and gawky
nails chewed
til they bleed
her head held down

she seldom speaks
having learned
to stay behind her eyes
no one can find her there
in that place
where her mind can turn
run barefoot
through the blue-eyed grass

it is for this child
who sees the world
through the long tunnels
of her eyes
it is for her

quills

we found our collie one cold morning
on the front steps an agony of quills
dad in the kitchen sweating and swearing
his fist of pliers
the collie's head held tight
too much inside the pain
i turn to run   to cover my ears
sit down dad says
where do you think you're going

now it is i
who pull quills from myself
dip them in ink
put them to paper

paper doll family

the child kneels
on the battleship linoleum
of the kitchen floor
scissors digging a ridge
into the thumb
of her left hand

she is cutting out
a family
from the Eaton's catalogue

mother does not need
operations
snipping
her away slowly
piece by piece
has time
for something other
than the patterns
of her pain

father does not
clip
his children
as if they were caraganas
needing
to be pruned back

the child cuts
out her family
carefully
her scissors
are sharp

a bitter word

it's not
that father
is a foreign language
or love
a bitter word
it's not
the spite he pelts out
in a hard rain
not the anger
that radiates off him
like a dry heat

it's if asked
i doubt he would know
the colour of my eyes

the butcher

the rasp of rain
against windows
as father hurls the meat
onto the scarred worktable
thick smell of blood
clotting the air

the muscle in his jaw
works back & forth
& back & forth
as he saws through bone

teeth clenched
he rips the saw
through pink flesh
grips the handle
so hard his knuckles
stand out white

lightning cleaves the shadows

what's amazing

is that it floats at all
a boat this rotted
should have sunk
long ago

there are no oars
no life-preservers
and bailing with beer bottles
is slow work

adrift in this leaky skiff
no one dares
to jump overboard
never having learned to swim

all too afraid
to stand
risk rocking the boat
bailing and bailing
and never in sight of shore

'57 Chevy

i see the car on a side-street
chrome glinting
in the afternoon sun
and suddenly it is summer
& i am seven again
& we are perched crosslegged
you & i
on the hood of father's '57 Chevy
holding huge watermelon smiles
seeing who can spit seeds farthest
into the august dust

i remember
when dad brought that car home
(pink & white
i loved the colour)
& how excited dad was
when he roused us from sleep
to take us for a ride
to the dairy queen

the two of us
snuggled into the soft leather seats
pyjama-clad & giggling
thrilled at this treat
of chocolate-dipped soft ice cream
& dad in a fine mood
winking at us in the rear-view mirror
reaching back to rumple your hair
and calling me lindy lou

& later at home
dad dancing mom around the kitchen
mom laughing & slapping at his shoulders
with a dishtowel & saying
bill stop it now stop it
but we knew
she didn't really want him to

changing a flat

my memory is the smell of hot
tar
the sticky august afternoon
at the road's edge
we do not play
but remain still
in the heat

mosquitoes tremble the air
above where father kneels
grunting
he wipes at sweat
the muscle in his jaw clenched
we watch quiet
make ourselves small

the tire iron slips
he spits obscenities
that sizzle
on hot pavement

we feel the beginnings of blisters
inside us
there is no shade

nancy

mother
friends say your name
like a small dance
on their tongues
they say
you were quietly pretty
recall your laugh
like summer rain

mother i would rather
they had said
you were a spitfire
with a quick-kindled temper
had grabbed life
been wild-spirited and splendid

lived your short time fiercely
going out
like a shooting star
blazing a parabola
across a midnight sky

nothing to be done

it was Mrs. Pritchard
taught the ninth grade Sunday School
good Presbyterian Mrs. Pritchard
with her small superior soul
her mind as stiff
as the starched cotton
of her husband's Sunday shirts

saw it as her place
to teach these young ones
the dangers
of flirting with the devil
to hold them up
before the divine displeasure
of her God
herself a sort of substitute
who sat in judgement
of their souls

but what
oh what was she to do
with that shameless girl Nancy
flaunting those bright red fingernails
that pouting scarlet mouth
painted up like a two dollar trollop
stained by satan himself
Nancy who looked straight
into the eyes of boys
Nancy with that self-satisfied
little half smile
taunting her

but there was nothing
to be done about it
nothing at all
and Mrs. Pritchard could only scold
with the disapproving weight of her eyes
the set of her lean lips
Nancy
the reverend's daughter

getting ready

when they told her
it was terminal
i remember thinking
it was like she was taking a trip
somewhere
& wanted to make sure
everything was looked after
while she was away

she showed me how
grandpa liked his tea
extra strong three sugars
where to go
to pay the power bill
to press dad's work shirts
collar first
how often to water the houseplants

getting ready to go
as if any minute
she would be packing up her suitcase
with her two good dresses
having dad drop her off
at the bus terminal
clutching a packet of peppermints
for the ride
with a nickel in her jacket pocket
to call home
from the other end

The Amazing Watson Sisters

i was eleven you six
we were The Amazing Watson Sisters
circus performers extraordinaire
in our imaginary spangled leotards
i airplaned you
high above my head
steadied you
on my shoulders
arms outstretched
the crowd clamoured

but now
i can no longer balance you
i feel you slip
losing your foothold
you must learn
as i have
everything depends on this:
keep a firm grip
do not look down

you wear laughter

sister
like bright diaphanous scarves
flung about your shoulders
they float behind you
flamboyant on the breeze

swirled in vivid ribbons
of laughter you move
through your days
a gay peacock play of colour

but sister
i look closely
and see the colours clash
against the whiteness
of your flesh

deny what's said
my sister
in your grey and solemn eyes

the yellow dress

we pretend we are somewhere else
out shopping or going for coffee
try not to notice
the sharp bite of disinfectant
that clings to the air
the narrow windows bolted across
with solid metal grates

you are wearing your favourite dress
the one with the yellow flowers
you said once
that it made you feel happy
every time you wore it
like putting on sunshine

a snarl of grey hair
in a tattered terry bathrobe
leans against the far wall
bangs her head slowly back and forth
each time striking the plaster
with a loud thump
your hand tightens on my arm

a man his red shirt unbuttoned
grins stump toothed
and yells hi hi hi
i look at you
your smile frozen
brave in your yellow dress

your room is bare
so bare
a narrow bed
a dresser
a closet
four hangers

guess i don't need
high heels here you say
then your smile breaks
wind rising in your eyes
you grab me   hang on to me
and nothing
not even the yellow dress
can stop the storm from coming now

breathing
(for my sister)

our childhood
was one
endless

held
breath
the very air
too dangerous
for breathing

our brother
held his breath
so often
and for so long
he finally forgot how
his small lungs bursting

I read once
the Inuit word
for breathe
is also the word
for poem

let these poems
be his breathing
yours and mine

smiling for dear life

i am posed beside you
in a navy sailor dress
you in blue velvet overalls
we have been
scrubbed and combed and dressed
and we are smiling for dear life

this picture
makes me ache for you
little brother
for all the times
you had to pretend and pretend
had to smile
until your face hurt
and all for the sake
of some false family

if you were here now
you wouldn't have to smile
about anything
although i like to think
one day as i have brother
you might have wanted to
you might have learned

again for david

you were a sailor
on a ship
that bore no Plimsoll line
to mark the safe load
it could bear

those you named
as friends unscrupulous
as the shipowners
who loaded the vessels down
knowing the ships might sink
and not caring
the crew could drown

the gift

do you remember that day dad
last summer
driving in to town
just the two of us
and you started
reminiscing
about that Christmas
so long ago now
when you and Hughie were boys
and set fire to the cordwood
grandpa livid
laying into you
with the leather belt
til grandma stepped in
grandpa raising the belt
and roaring "get outa the way
or i'll hit you too"

so now it's another Christmas
and maybe i can't quite forgive you
your broken love
but i can understand
a little now
your huge rage
though i know
you're far past healing
i can give you only
this birth of understanding
this small gift

it is because

inside
you are still
the same skinny-legged boy
with freckles
i knew at sixteen
who slow danced with me
to Hey Jude
that summer night
at the Terrace Gardens
under a kaleidoscope
of christmas lights
on a sawdust-sprinkled floor

and it is because
we walked barefoot on the beach
you swinging my sandals
on the fingers of one hand
and the night was magical
loons calling their promises
across a lake like black velvet
and i pretended to stumble
and the tremble of your hands
on the waist of my cotton dress
and the sweet corniness
of you telling me
i was more beautiful than the moon

the most beautiful poems

she has ever known
he has hand-
written
on the small of her back
their telling
traced
along her belly
skin of her inner thigh

my son is missing

someone stole him
while he was waiting
for the bus
he's been gone
since he was fourteen
i haven't called the police
i keep thinking
maybe he'll show up

i posted his school picture
in Safeway in case
someone recognizes him
sometimes if i look quickly
out of the corner of my eye
i think i see him

and there are signs
his clothes in the hamper
his bed usually slept in
once i met someone
in the hall
who looked like him
though i wasn't sure

mother and son dancing

in this one
taken at your wedding
we are dancing
how strange
to be held in your arms
i who always held you
too close
like a miser keeps his treasure

sometimes i wanted you
to be three again
sleeping in my arms
the years
when i hugged you
you would cringe away from me
those years of distance
i hadn't bargained for
had to store my embraces
packed away
like winter clothes
folded into an old trunk

i remember you
so scared that day
struggling
between laugher and tears
you've always hated that
feeling somehow less a man
because you cry so easily

in this picture we dance
i in your arms
somewhere beyond us the music
and we are smiling together
you and i at something
like a secret shared

far and away

in the Black Hills
of Northern Ireland
in County Monahan
lie your roots
my son
in that green country
of your grandparents' birth

Shawn we called you
a fine corker of an Irish name
and i wouldn't doubt
if far back
there wasn't another
Shawn Monahan
your great great great grandfather say

and i wonder
if he'd have been like you
tall and strong
with a temper just like yours
i wonder if he'd have had your passion
that Shawn from long ago
if you'd have met as friends

some day son
i hope you travel there
to the north of Ireland
to County Monahan
to stand upon the soil
where once that young man stood
see with your own eyes, my son
the things he saw
and touch that other Shawn
the Ireland that's in you

being invisible

isn't easy
i keep crashing into people
who don't even notice
i've knocked them over

seems like
whenever i speak
there is somebody saying
exactly what i've just said
but in ten thousand more words

i've tried wearing bright colours
spandex dresses
my dangliest earrings
snapping gum in people's ears
but still i remain unseen

there's got to be some way
to become more visible
spray-paint myself
Day-Glo orange
wrap Christmas tree lights
around my legs
and take up riding a Harley

solitaire

she sheds her dress
and standing bare
thinks of the coldest thing
she knows   the coldest thing

and she takes a cloth
and polishes
her arms and legs
her belly and her breasts
shines and shines herself
til she is all sparkling surfaces

until she is as hard as diamond
as clean and chill
and crystalline
she is a solitaire
her fire frozen deep within
where nothing can break
nothing can touch her now

she glitters
like ice in a winter sun
her many facets
mirroring everything

poultice

why don't you smile
any more
he asks her
smile
he says

as if he were offering
an old-fashioned remedy
like the bread-and-sugar poultices
her mother would lay on her wounds

as if by simply smiling
she might heal herself
make it all better
the infection drawn

a brown study

come
close your eyes
almost smell the scent
of cinnamon
of cardamom and coriander
savour the flavour
of bittersweet chocolate

hear the mellow sound
of brown
let its music
slide over you

imagine
the opulent gleam
of old mahogany
musty light filtering
through a cobwebbed window

say ochre, sorrel, burnt sienna

now picture a woman
suncoppered skin bare
beneath a gown
of coffee-coloured silk

she is a brown study:
an absorption
a preoccupation
etched in sepia
she is the colour of contemplation
a study in brown

camouflage

it's inherited you know
this being invisible
passed on to me
by my mother, my grandmother
handed down
like the family photos
from one generation
to the next
this ability
to go about unnoticed

in those photos
i do look like them
same brown hair brown eyes
we blend into backgrounds
too easily
a camouflage perhaps
a way of hiding

like deer
at the road's edge
standing so still
you might never
have seen them at all

living inside out

she finds herself
wearing her centre
right at the surface
too sensitive to all this light

she is searching for a skin
thick and tough
as the dandelions
that take her lawn come spring
a skin
sturdy as the rubber suits
her husband wears for diving

or a skin perhaps
tough as an old alligator suitcase
like the leathery hide
of the iguana
she remembers tied to a fence post
in that market in mexico

she should like
a skin   that strong

taper

she
can't
believe
no one notices
her hair
caught
on fire
this way
can't believe
that no one
sees her
burning
a tall blue
taper
waiting
in a window

the cinnamon moths

it's not
the august night
that she remembers
not the breeze
that soughed against her skin
like watered silk
nor is it the moon
that she remembers
all tangled in the branches
of the ornamental apple

it's the cinnamon moths
she can't forget
the cinnamon moths
bunting their soft bodies
over and over
against the summer screen
it's the cinnamon moths
that move inside her
the delicate shapes
of their desire

sometimes he sees her

standing at the window
just standing there
so still
in the evening light

as if she were listening
to some faint and far off song
inside her
its quiet cadence

he feels her
moving away from him
moving to that music
singing to herself
over and over

the words
she cannot teach him
to a song
he will never know

Mijas

remember that day
rain a dove grey veil
when we stepped off the bus
in Mijas
that upholstered American woman
steaming on ahead of us
complaining about the rain
her little husband
hauled along in her wake
we are laughing   the two of us
at her   at this fine rain
and in delight
at the marvel
of this little mountain town

we roam the steep and narrow streets
browsing for trinkets
to take back home
the village rises all around us
gleaming white
balconies flamboyant with flowers
and everywhere the scent of Spain
the smell of fires
the peppery tang of cooking

in a doorway
an old woman
gives me her shy smile
at her side
a small boy peeks out
from the folds of her skirts
his brown eyes laughing
in the esplanade
we find a little galeria

over coffee and churros
all afternoon we watch the rain
and one another

i think this
the most wonderful rain
and Mijas a place of such magic
i can't remember
ever being happier
or more in love with you
oh Mijas Mijas
where are you now
where is the laughter?
where is that rain?

almost wanting

outside the fire
she dances   always
she dances
just outside the fire

heat kissing her skin
as she twirls
bare legs flashing
in the firelight

through the dark air
sparks leap and settle
clasps for her flying hair

faster she dances
faster still
incandescent now
the fire flares

small hands reach out
to touch her twisting feet
hungry flames wanting her
the undisguised desire of fire

nearer she dances
nearer still
almost wanting the fire
to take her   almost wanting
to feel that burn

a slow dance

she is the distant blaze
you see on orange-mooned
October nights
across a field the flames
shifting
stuttering the shadows

a bonfire
she bursts
a shower of embers
that spiral up
against a darkening sky

sometimes
she is candlewick
is kindling
at times
she feels like matches
tossed into a wind

how easily
she takes the shape of fire
has always been
a slow dance in the flames

how did it happen

lovers don't finally meet somewhere.
they're in each other all along
– Rumi (1207-1273)

how did it happen
that you came in
through a door
i hadn't known
i had left open
and in your quiet eyes
i saw and touched
the stillness in myself

spun glass

we make conversation
out of anything
talk of weather
work
the cost of a cup of coffee
our words carefully
not touching

what we really
want to say
turns slowly
in the spaces
left between our words
turns slowly
in the air between us
as delicate
as spun glass

you are in me

like the little hoof prints
white-tailed deer
have left in the night
set into the sidewalk
in front of the Lakeview Hotel
by morning
too late
to be smoothed over

the only voice

don't worry
nothing is going to happen

it's just wind-dabbled water
a bit of pebbly beach
edged by a line
of long-limbed pine
gulls sculling
in a watercolour sky

nothing to it
at all really
just:
the lake
trees
white birds overhead

not a thing
to make you think of me
if you closed your eyes
it could be
as if
i wasn't even here

the only voice
you hear
is the sound
small waves make
shush shushing
against the shore

dark eyes

absorb light
refuse surfaces
look into everything
too deeply
past what's visible
are always
falling in
always going under

dark eyes
fathom what the heart knows
winnow out
some secret inside part
of you
are always
falling in
always
going under

river of silence

there is a river of silence
that flows through you

i pan it for gold

the bends

if i could
i would dive down
and drag you up
to the surface
tow you
into the light

it would be
no slow safe ascent

you have descended
into that dark ocean
so deep
and for so long
there would be pain
it wouldn't be easy
something i suppose
like getting the bends

but you'd have no choice
you'd have to feel it
you'd have to feel everything

tides

she paints a stark scene
black rags of clouds
a grey and wind-rocked sea
there is a man on the shore
he is the only colour
a splash of yellow rainjacket
where he stands
face turned

he watches the long waves
their constant pull
watches them
crest and break
crest and break
perhaps no one sees it
but she paints the tide there
rising in his eyes

five minutes of hail

we have spent years
you and i
in our perfect
white-painted picket-fence lives
tending our neat little gardens
our children
grown tall as early corn
our marriages
as comfortable as pumpkins

i look at you
knowing
what could so easily happen
knowing
we could be
like five minutes of hail

desire

and he is undoing the zip on her white dress and telling her how beautiful her back is and she is thinking of this moment as a poem she hasn't written yet about desire and where it goes and why

and even the word is a slow hot ache inside you malleable as butter as wax undulating down like blood within your body desire is a dream journey we travel to places we will never go beneath an imagined sun exotic as Moroccan orange

desire is everything at the wrong moment a knowing and not knowing a hummingbird's fierce thrum desire is an argument your heart makes it thinks there is an answer when there was never any question

and some things have no end to them some things you carry like a talisman inside you all this hunger you never knew you had and it was fire we never called it that but it was all that's left is our wanting to burn

and at night desire lies naked beside you it won't let you sleep its hands are everywhere

cinnabar

i dreamt
i was a dark continent
somewhere
you'd never been before
with a name
that drummed in your blood
like Marrakech or Zanzibar

a place
of verdant valleys
lush and green
with grotto ferns
where waterfalls fanned down
to azure pools
and toucans called
from the tamarind trees

and the heat of my sun
was saffron
poured over your skin
and everywhere around you
the scent of sandalwood and cinnabar

nightly

the island unfolds
between sea and sky
island of sunswollen days
where her body flowered
beneath his
like bougainvillea
in a shimmer of tropic heat

her sleeping body stirs
succumbs
to the slowflowing island dream
of his breath across her
caress of trade winds
she opens
to the hot hands of sun

a woman dreams

she gathers kindling
strikes wooden matches
against her nipples
builds a bonfire
between her breasts
her body turned touchwood

quickly the blaze spreads
her limbs are burning branches
flames fingering her throat
her face crackles
lips teeth tongue

a woman dreams
somewhere deep inside
the fury
within the very heart of her
always this stillness
always this calm
at the centre of her fire

the naked woman

comes out of nowhere
on her little bare feet
she won't stay
decently covered
won't leave
her clothes on
no matter the weather
no matter what anyone thinks

the naked woman
needs to feel
she needs to feel
the cold rush of rain
like ice water
rinsing her clear
needs to feel
the sun's hot copper hands
to dance unconfined
in blue columns of moonlight

she doesn't want garments
to get in the way
wants to live life
unclad
with nothing hidden
to stand
full in sunlight
unrestricted
and raw as October
her hair
haloing in the wind

for Joshua (at two)

in your world
there is only
your small self
everything is *mine*
you tell me
your dark eyes demanding

one day
you will understand
what has taken me
this long to learn

listen little one:
do not desire too much
too desperately
some things can not be yours
no matter how much you want them

you can not have the moon
my darling
you do not own the sky

woman within

who are you anyway
woman with your words
you cannot restrict me
to your poems
i would never stay
within your boundaries
i leap out at the edges

i won't be confined
by the cages
of your words
won't be defined
by what you try
to make of me
what you pretend to know

the prattle of your poems
can never hold me
wrapped in a language
i am so much bigger than

all your little syllables
will never level me
you cannot
write me down to size

bare wood

i don't want
these poems
hewn from hard
unvarnished truths
these poems
that will not
be whitewashed
why is it
i must always
name everything?

so much in me
sanded down
unfinished

you leave me

with nothing i can say
words pinned
quivering inside

if i could
i would set them free
like small blue butterflies
send them trembling
into your hands

i remember my mother
telling me once
not to touch
the wings of butterflies
or they would no longer fly

you take away
this much of me

you touch my wings

of dreams & dragonflies

it is said
in the last century
there were people
who believed dragonflies
were the devil's darning needles
would sew the lips
of those who told tales

sometimes
i dream the danger
a blur of blue-black wings
and wake
to find phrases
falling backward
down my throat
my mouth a smooth seam

arctic man

he has never been
to Baffin Island
never set foot
in Frobisher Bay
but he understands
this landscape
of savage cold
and sudden summers

he feels the wind
bend him
like a kayak rib
in the long north night
hears wolves
wail to a bitter moon

his breath breaks
within this cell
of ice and snow
he denies this nothingness
inside him
a slowness
only the arctic seems to know

winter of words

i am caught
in this winter of words
they dance round each other
like fast-falling snowflakes
your words
are cold kisses
caught in my hair

snow-blind
i stumble ahead
my stung eyes
the words falling
in frozen flowers
round me everywhere

i am so lost
out here so cold
the drifts are piling up
closing me
in their soft white caul

chimera

perhaps we are
a mirage on the blacktop
you and i
floating hazy and surreal
on the horizon
an optical illusion
a distortion
and nothing more

we have no reference point
nothing tangible
nothing to hold on to
some things
are just your imagination
what seems so real
is so often not

a chimera
a dream you cannot touch
there are no lakes on the highway
you just get there
and they're gone

thin as rain

where you are
it's always
raining
around   inside you
its cool blue breath

where i am
this slender rain
like shot silver
behind my eyes
like a tunnel
that has no end

on your tongue
the taste of nothing
rain a veil
that hides your mourning

and i'm falling
through my fingers
thin as rain

trains

she wished him
steaming trains
that left
from winter stations

slow trains
chuffing their way
past stark silhouettes
of poplar stands and pine
through snow banks
blue in moonlight

she wished him
old-fashioned trains
trundling
over wooden trestles
whistling lonely
on night winds
writing their way
across the winter wheat fields

she wished him
midnight trains
to carry him
beyond the ice and snow
beyond this barren countryside
to that destination
deep inside
that green and fertile
province of the heart

where blue whales swim

lying naked
where blue whales swim
on the far blue horizon
she dreams
salt water foaming
about her thighs
her hair trailing
seaweed on the little waves
behind her

dreams she is
swimming out to meet them
swimming out
to where the blue whales move
in their graceful ancient dance

their bodies sliding
through the dark blue water
surrounding her   touching her
with their cool sensitive skin

she dreams
her own body
as ancient and beautiful
dreams she belongs in their element
in the sea's slow dance
she longs to feel
what the blue whales feel
charting places
few have ever dreamed of
going with them
to wherever it is
the blue whales go

in all that grey

i was wrong
though i didn't know it then
didn't know
grey was a colour
you could never comprehend

you who could only see
in black and white
and i
always in between
always given
to varying shades of grey
like mist on a still river
i moved beyond you

you could never see me
for i was simply smoke
or shadow
in the pewter afternoon
a shape as indistinct
as dreaming

there was only my voice
to tell you i was there
only my voice
in all that grey

no refunds

i would take back
this loving
return
where it came from
but i've lost
the receipt now
too late for it
anyway
i would take back
this loving
you don't really
want it   no room
for it anywhere
your house
is already confused
and too crowded

my love will get left
in a box
in your basement
like the niagara falls lamp
your grandmother gave you
like the old wicker chair
that nobody wants

you were a season

that fell somewhere
between winter and spring
a season of contradictions

some days
a cold wind
shouldering its way
through the trees

some days
there were heat waves
shimmering off everything

i never knew
what to expect
of your weather

i never knew
how i should dress

somewhere

snow geese
signal in the dark
rise up
from the ice-bound lake
inside her
like woodsmoke
on a january morning

sudden flurry
of white birds wheeling
on the cold blue crests of air

beneath an icicle moon
they turn
and leave her now
fleeing swiftly south

toasting spring

ice lays
delicate lace
across the lake
listen
to the crystal
toasting spring
above us

a chandelier of moon

Acknowledgements

The author wishes to thank Lorna Crozier, who taught me so much, Patrick Lane for helping find an order, Elizabeth Philips for her editorial comments and valuable criticism, the Sage Hill Writing Experience and the members of sans noms poetry group who witnessed the birth of many of these poems. Special thanks to my husband Don Monahan for his love and steady encouragement and to Jack Hicks for his hugs.

Earlier versions of some of these poems have appeared in the following literary publications: *Grain, Other Voices, Transition, Zygote, University of Saskatchewan Sheaf,* and *Museletters.* The first lines of the poems "trains" and "where blue whales swim" are based on lines taken from the book *The Bridges of Madison County* by Robert James Waller.

about the author

Lynda Monahan has published her poetry in literary periodicals such as *Grain, Other Voices* and *Museletters*, and had it broadcast on CBC Radio. *a slow dance in the flames* is her first published poetry collection.

Lynda Monahan was born in Prince Albert and has lived there most of her life. She currently divides her time between that city and Waskesiu. She teaches creative writing at the Saskatchewan Institute of Applied Science and Technology (SIAST) in Prince Albert.

THE OPEN EYE POETRY SERIES:

Poetry that knows where you live!

Check out the rest of the titles in the 1998 Open Eye series:

My Flesh the Sound of Rain
Heather MacLeod

A masterpiece of native and white myth and icon – an Indian shaman shares attention with the Christian Virgin and the pagan holy days Beltain and Samhain.

Second Skin
Jeanne Marie de Moissac

Poetry born of an attachment to earth's abundance – children, animals both domestic and wild, plants and stones of the rural landscape.

Sex, Death and Naked Men
Bernice Friesen

Sex, death, religion – the big questions, taken in sassy, ribald, in-your-face broadsides, or tender, tentative, thoughtful lyrics.

COTEAU BOOKS